Wonders
in the
PATH
WAY

AMAZING REVELATION OF EXTRAORDINARY
WONDERS OF GOD IN THE PATHWAY

DAVID SAA FATORMA, JR.

FIRST WORD
PUBLISHING CO

This book is dedicated solely to my Heavenly Father, the almighty God ELOHIM, through whom all the mysteries and inexplicable testimonies contain in this book were made possible. I am forever grateful to ELOHIM who has been my sustainer over the years and without the shadow of doubt takes the credit and glory for all that I am.

ACKNOWLEDGEMENTS

I want to acknowledge Dr. Prince Maurice Parker, a dear friend, a professor of theology and pastor, who I have known for the past two decades and half. My first encounter with him was when he visited Liberia in 1999 to speak at a church conference here in Monrovia, Liberia.

At that conference, I grabbed a revelation that he released while teaching that I used over the years that helped me in my many years of ministerial experience. When speaking at the leaders' conference, Dr. Parker indicated that every vision has three stages: "the birth, the death, and the supernatural resurrection." With that revelation in mind, we navigated through those different stages of our own vision safely because we were informed and never surprised at every level.

When I took on the challenge to write this book, I knew I had to reach a point of editing and when I reached that point, I ran to Dr. Parker for help, and he took on the challenge without any hesitation just as he did with my last book.

I am so full of gratitude for the sacrifices made by him to get this book completed and available for all of us. Of course, words cannot express my gratitude Dr. Parker you are truly a blessing to this generation.

TABLE OF CONTENTS

FOREWORD

D avid Saa Fatorma, Jr. is the General Overseer of the Light Streams Chapel Solution Outreach Ministries, and an emerging leader in the kingdom building and expansion with extraordinary and supernatural experiences that is mind blowing and his testimonial book will fill your heart with faith and hope in Jesus. I have come to know him over the years as a serious kingdom ambassador who is full of fire for kingdom building and believes in looking beyond his circle to network with other Christian leaders to get the job done.

He and his beautiful wife are great role model and example to the body of Christ in Liberia where he is stationed by the Lord. Pastor David Fatorma is a not only survivor of a massacre which happened during the 15-years civil war in Liberia, but he is a message from God to our generation that easily wants to give up on God and try other gods. He is a living, breathing and walking miracle on planet earth declaring that our God is omnipotent and faithful.

Emerging young leaders are being birthed today with very promising potential and hope for the future church locally and globally. Pastor David Fatorma whom I have come to know and experience his ministry and life is one of the young leaders that is not just a leader but has leadership skills and ability and the fear of God. His ministries impact on the body of Christ in Liberia and through the media is raising more interest in people to want to know more about his faith and love for Jesus. His incredible understanding, and insight in the scripture about God and his mighty works can be highly appreciated as Pastor David expressed them in his powerful book, Wonders in the Pathway.

It's an exciting, mind blowing and heart captivating book which will transform your life and make you forever a believer in the faithfulness of God. This book makes one to see and become more curious to study in depth about everything God has shown him to write. The revelation he has about the wonders in creation in the scriptures and His moving story about how God rescued him out of the hands of the rebels by divine interventions speaks of God's purpose and power to bring to pass his plans for Pastor David. Unusual miracles in the whole process of him escaping the rebels line during the brutal Liberian civil war reveals the awesomeness of our God.

I highly recommend this book to be read and used for teaching purposes, small groups, and leadership conferences etc. It is fully packed with many life changing revelations of God's supernatural interventions, and practical demonstration of His power. This book will raise your faith level and strengthen you when you face trials as a disciple of Jesus. David illustrates his experiences of God's grace, mercy, love and care in a way that makes it very simple and clear.

His travels to the United States and how God used him in visions and dreams is faith building and accurate. He has an unusual anointing and I respect his stance for righteousness and truth. "*Many are the afflictions of the righteous, but the Lord delivers him out of them all*" (Psalm 34:19 KJV). This scripture verse is powerfully fulfilled in his trials and the attacks he went through.

His humility in recognizing the hand of God and giving him the glory in his walk of faith truly tells you that he is Christ centered. I can relate to his stories when I think of the times I had my own near death experience as I came close to being killed during civil war. Several times I was put at gun point but they could not get at me. The Lord's divine intervention was so powerful that up to now I feel I am a wonder.

Finally my brethren, please grab a copy of this powerful life changing book and read these true and powerful testimonies and I can assure you without any shadow of doubt that your faith will catapult to another level after reading this book. Remember that each of us in this Christian journey will one day be tested and tried. A book as such should serve as a means of encouragement and strength.

Evangelist Jospeh Billy Bimba

Founder and President of Billy Bimba Global Ministries Inc., USA

Founder and President of Liberia for Jesus Evangelistic Ministries Inc., Republic of Liberia

INTRODUCTION

A s the Lord impresses upon my heart to write a third book to record purpose and archive some of the amazing wonders I have encountered since answering the call to ministry, I recently had the opportunity to visit Zambia on an invitation from the "Christian Business Men Connection" (CBMC Africa), of which I serve as Liberia's Country Director, to attend a leaders conference in Lusaka.

After the leaders' summit, I had the privilege to visit Livingstone, the tourist city of Zambia, where one of the Seven Wonders of the World is situated, the Victoria Waterfalls, which attracts thousands of tourists from around the world to encounter and come in touch with the remarkable wonders of God's creation.

I was amazed when our team visited Living Stone Park the day before visiting the falls. We toured the park and found animals such as hippopotamuses, chimpanzees, monkeys, rhinos, deer, zebras, giraffes, and much more moving freely about their daily routines. What amazes me is the fact that as we drove and, at some point, walked through the park, we experienced a peaceful environment. It is not seeing the animals that fascinates me, but the fact that we could walk freely among them without being hurt as they went about their own business. This reminds me of the wonders of God's creation. When God first created the world, Adam and Eve lived freely and harmoniously with all those beasts, some of which I consider very dangerous today.

Then came the second day of our tour, when we encountered one of the most notable Seven Wonders of the World, which makes

Zambia and Africa famous. As we drew closer to Victoria Falls, we heard a terrific noise from the fall, which welcomes its visitors. Moving forward, we were amazed at the first sight of the waterfalls. A friend said, "Victoria Falls can only be experienced and not described." This saying is a true definition of a Wonder: experienced, not described.

While it cannot be described in totality because of its extraordinary nature, let me hint at what I experienced. It is a massive body of water falling hundreds of feet from the top of the fall into the Zambezi River. The presence of the rainbow, and this time it is not in the skies but in the center of the waterfall, was mind-blowing for me. The constant splashes of water all over us, like the fall of rain as we toured, were also spectacular. Indeed, God is astonishing in His marvelous creation.

Meanwhile, I am pleased to present "Wonders in the Pathway," my third book. This book captures details of the wonders of God in my life and ministry over the last 30 years. I have seen the hand of God work wonders indescribable, and I am inclined to bring to you in detail His notable works over the years. In my first book, After His Touch, I presented the details of my experience of miraculously surviving a massacre in 1993 at age 17. I want to report that since that experience, I have also seen countless miracles in the pathway, as I have seen many other supernatural interventions of God that need to be told. John declares, "*And they overcame him by the blood of the Lamb, and by the word of their testimony,*" (Revelation 12:11).

I pray that the testimonies in this book will elevate your faith to the point that your life will be transformed as you will also experience God's supernatural intervention.

CHAPTER ONE

THE GOD OF WONDER

God is the God of wonders, and His nature reveals His wonders from creation and throughout all generations. The inexplicable nature of the wonders of God cannot be overemphasized, and this is made manifest even in his natural creation. Hence, in this chapter, I am inclined to talk about the natural manifestation of the wonders of God. Meanwhile, I urge you to tighten your seat belt as we take off through this journey to discover the inexplicable wonders of God, beginning from this chapter to the final chapter of this book.

HIS EVERLASTING NATURE SPEAKS WONDERS

First, have you wondered about the self-existence of God? From childhood to adulthood, there were moments when I sat quietly and wondered about the eternity of God. The everlasting and self-existence nature of God blows my mind. God is God all by himself. He is the rock of ages; from everlasting to everlasting, He remains supreme. He is the uncaused cause and the unmoved mover. It's remarkable to know that there is someone who has been there forever, which speaks to the fact that life did not begin because of the Big Bang as evolutionists project it, but that there is eternal hope beyond this short life's journey of ours in this universe.

Let's look at this Scripture: *"Before the mountains were born, you brought forth the whole world, from everlasting to everlasting, you are God."* (Psalm 90:2 NIV). Before the creation of the universe, He was already from everlasting to everlasting; thus, there is no room for doubt, nor is there any space for the pundits, the evolutionists, and their Big Bang Theory. Yes, our heavenly father is the everlasting God.

It is important to note that there is a designer behind every design. Because this is an undeniable fact, we can say without any shadow of a doubt that our beautiful universe was created by the greatest of all designers, the almighty God. To accept that every beautiful architectural work has an architect but refuse to accept that this beautifully designed universe has a chief architect is double standards, sad, and pitiful.

Let's look at some Scriptures that speak to the creative nature of God: *"When I consider your heavens the work of your fingers, the moon, and the stars, which you have set in place."* (Psalm 8:3 NIV).

Here, the psalmist speaks to the wonder of considering the creation of the heavens, the moon, and the stars all by the fingers of God. How breathtaking this is; indeed, God is the greatest designer. We are told, *"In the beginning, God created the heavens and the earth"* (Genesis 1:1 NIV). There is absolutely no doubt that God is the creator, the inventor, and designer of this universe and everything in it.

The wonders of God's creation go way beyond the creation of just the universe, as it's important to mention that every living creature is the handiwork of God, the master designer. *"I will praise you because I am fearfully and wonderfully made; your works are wonderful; I know that full well."* (Psalm 139:14). In this verse, the psalmist continues his recognition of the wonders of God through His creation. As he looks at himself, the psalmist realizes that God has fearfully and wonderfully made him and everything else in creation.

All around us, around the world, and every day, we see the wonders of the mighty hand of God in full display. When you look at the sun, it rises in the morning and goes down by the evening, which continues to happen from the day of creation without any interruption whatsoever. At night, there is a wonder of the moon and stars that give us natural light. Oh, how amazing that is! Irrespective of its massive body of water and force, the oceans and seas have limits that prevent an overflow of water everywhere. If this is not a wonder, I don't know what else would be.

Our next chapter will focus on some extraordinary wonders of Jesus' earthly ministry.

CHAPTER TWO

EXTRAORDINARY WONDERS OF JESUS' EARTHLY MINISTRY

A s we progress in our discussions of wonders in the pathway, it is crucial to take a break and take a retrospective view of some extraordinary wonders Jesus encountered in His earthly ministry. I firmly believe that these outstanding wonders occurred not just for the glorification of God but that, individually, our faiths should be lifted to a point where we can experience the wonders. The Bible declares, *"and they overcame him because of the blood of the Lamb, and because of the Word of their testimony…"* (Revelation 12:11 KJV).

The miraculous testimonies of Jesus' earthly ministry will enable us to overcome our problems today, bearing in mind that He is the same yesterday, today, and forever. If it happened yesterday, greater things would happen today, just as he had promised. *"Very truly, I tell you, whoever believes in me will do the works I have been doing, and they will do even greater things than these because I am going to the Father."* (John 14:12 NIV).

To begin with, let's look at the resurrection of Jesus himself, which is arguably the greatest of all miracles because He laid down his life and yet rose from the grave after three days in the grave. It is one thing for one to raise the dead and do exceptional miraculous wonders. For example, Jesus raised a man from the grave after four days of death, which is on our list of extraordinary miracles; however, for one to lay down his own and take it back is an unmatched miracle. This miracle was pivotal to the formation of the new covenant church; imagine if Christ had not been resurrected.

Listen to this:

And behold, there was a great earthquake: for the angel of the Lord descended from heaven and came and rolled back the stone from the door and sat upon it. His countenance was like lightning, and his raiment white as snow: And for fear of him, the keepers did shake and became as dead men. And the angel answered and said unto the women, Fear not ye: for I know that ye seek Jesus, which was crucified. He is not here, for he is risen, as he said. Come, see the place where the Lord lay. And go quickly and tell his disciples that he is risen from the dead; and behold, he goeth before you into Galilee; there shall ye see him: lo, I have told you.

MATTHEW 28:2-7, KJV

Praise God! What an astounding miracle this is! Nothing else like this has ever been recorded. Mohamed, the prophet of Islam who claimed to be sent by God, died, and that was the end of the story. Bahaullah, a self-proclaimed prophet of the Bahá'í faith, died, and that was the end of his story. Siddhārtha Gautama, most commonly referred to as the Buddha, the founder of the Buddhist faith, for the Buddhists, died and never rose from the grave, but thank God that our Lord voluntarily laid down his life, and in three days, He took it back as He rose from the grave, and death couldn't hold him captive.

Earlier on, I mentioned that a man was raised for the dead after four days; yes, Jesus did raise Lazarus from the grave, having been dead for four days. What an exceptional miracle that was. Let's look at what the Scripture says about this miracle:

> *Jesus said, Take ye away the stone. Martha, the sister of him that was dead, saith unto him, Lord, by this time he stinketh: for he hath been dead four days. Jesus saith unto her, Said I not unto thee, that, if thou wouldest believe, thou shouldest see the glory of God? Then they took away the stone from the place where the dead was laid. And Jesus lifted up his eyes, and said, Father, I thank thee that thou hast heard me. And I knew that thou hearest me always: but because of the people which stand by I said it, that they may believe that thou hast sent me. And when he thus had spoken, he cried with a loud voice, Lazarus, come forth. And he that was dead came forth, bound hand and foot with grave clothes: and his face was bound about with a napkin. Jesus saith unto them, Loose him, and let him go.*

JOHN 11:39-44, KJV

What a fantastic miracle! A man died, and after four days, he was resurrected. Even his family, in their hopelessness, tried to prevent Christ from attempting to raise him from the dead, claiming that he was already dead for four days and was decomposing. But Jesus went ahead and raised him from the dead.

How about the ascension wonder? This was not just the last miracle of Jesus' earthly ministry but an event that brought closure to his earthly ministry. This is a reminder that Jesus' arrival on earth was a remarkable wonder, as he was conceived by the Virgin Mary. This was an outstanding miracle that had never been seen nor heard of throughout history up to this date.

Listen to this:

> But after he had considered this, an angel of the Lord appeared to him in a dream and said, "Joseph, son of David, do not be afraid to take Mary home as your wife because what is conceived in her is from the Holy Spirit.
>
> MATTHEW 1:20 NIV

Meanwhile, while Jesus' arrival was marked by an outstanding wonder, it will interest you to know that similarly, his departure was nothing short of another mind-blowing wonder in broad daylight in the view of his disciples as he physically ascended into heaven. After he said this, he was taken up before their very eyes, and a cloud hid him from their sight. They were looking intently into the sky as he was going when suddenly, two men dressed in white stood beside them:

"Men of Galilee," they said, "After he said this, he was taken up before their very eyes, and a cloud hid him from their sight. They were looking intently up into the sky as he was going, when suddenly two men dressed in white stood beside them. *"Men of Galilee," they said, "why do you stand here looking into the sky? This same Jesus, who has been taken from you into heaven, will come back in the same way you have seen him go into heaven.""* (Acts 1:9-11 NIV).

These extraordinary wonders of Jesus' earthly ministry and many more are evidence of the power and blessings available to the church today. Remember, Jesus said: *"Very truly, I tell you, whoever believes in me will do the works I have been doing, and they will do even greater things than these because I am going to the Father."* (John 14:12 NIV).

It is time we recognized our authority in Christ and took up the mantle left by Christ to live a victorious and wonderful Christian life.

CHAPTER THREE

REVELATIONAL WONDER

"*And afterward, I will pour out my Spirit on all people. Your sons and daughters will prophesy, your old men will dream dreams, your young men will see visions.*" (Joel 2:28 NIV). This passage of Scripture talks about the prophetic word of the Lord through Joel the prophet a promise from God to pour his spirit on all flesh in the last days, a dispensation we are currently into, to the extent that sons and daughters are prophesying, visions are being seen by young men and the older men are dreaming.

We are living in a day and age wherein prophetic revelation has a massive bearing on the church of Jesus Christ, as this gift plays a vital role in the day-to-day life of the church in all parts of the world. However, it is also important to note that this subject is very controversial as many false prophets have risen, causing controversies in the church. I was reminded by a good friend, Bishop Joseph Johnson III, one day while discussing a related topic on our Voice of the Church TV program about the many false prophets that have emerged in the church world, said:

Imagine that from the days of King Ahab, there were four hundred false prophets who prophesied lies to the king. Considering that from that period until now, hundreds of thousands, if not millions, are in our pulpits, leading the children of God astray.

While it is true that many false prophets parading the corridors of the church today cause harm, tearing families, churches, and friends apart instead of edifying the church, which is the actual essence of this beautiful gift, millions of genuine sons and daughters of God have been operating in this gift since the day of Pentecost, thereby fulfilling the promise of Joel 2:28.

This chapter aims to share experiences and testimonies of the wonders of revelation in my personal life and ministry. I trust they will bless you and encourage you to position yourself for revelational wonders.

REVELATIONAL WONDER TO SAFETY

To begin with, I would like to share with you the revelational wonder I experienced in 1993 when the Lord delivered me from a massacre that took the lives of others as they were brutally murdered, primarily by beheading. But the Lord intervened and spared my life while in the process of being beheaded. Some of you may know that I have written a book on my survival, and in that book, I mentioned one of the revelations. However, there is a revelation I did not mention in that book, which I learned recently from Ma Esther, who was part of our church in Liberia. She is a minister in training and an aid to my spiritual father, who I got separated from on the day that rebels launched an attack on

Zorzor Lofa County, as some church members and I fled to a nearby village to seek refuge.

I am told by Esther that my deceased spiritual father had requested that a fast and prayer be held for three days for all of us from the church who were considered missing because of the attack. She explained that during the fast and prayer, she had a dream she saw me running towards them, and in my hands were palm leaves. She testified that after explaining the dream, it did not take long before military men had come from Guinea to fetch them.

When I wasn't beheaded like the others, even though attempts were made, the Lord miraculously intervened. Even still, afterward, I was shot as I ran from the village. Nevertheless, the Lord again protected me from every single bullet. The next day, the Lord took me to Guinea under miraculous circumstances. Because, humanly speaking, there is no way I would have walked that distance by myself to Guinea with all the wounds I sustained during the attack, as I was severely wounded and bleeding profusely.

Fast-forward, I miraculously landed in Guinea, a country I had never been to, and on a road in that thick forest through which I had never traveled. Nevertheless, I found myself in Guinea, and I was taken to a clinic in the city of Koinyama overnight. The men who took me there returned to their village without adequately accounting for or providing any information about the patient they brought to them. The following day, the nurses and doctors had no clue who the patient was, and there needed to be more clarity about how I got in there in the first place.

The situation was complicated by the fact that I was no longer talking due to the severity of my injuries. To complicate the situation further, Guinea is a French-speaking country, and even if I could speak it, I would not have been able to communicate clearly.

So, talking to them in English wouldn't have helped me. However, some refugees who had fled Liberia because of the war recognized me and told the Guineans that I was a non-combatant in Liberia because the assumption was that I was a fighter. The military was called in to verify.

Meanwhile, those who recognized me at the clinic told the soldiers I was the son of a pastor who stayed in Liberia and couldn't flee, confirming that I wasn't a combatant. Furthermore, the evening of the same day this was happening, Esther had this dream, and the soldiers who weren't satisfied with the story given by my fellow refugees chose to cross the border in Liberia to confirm if I truly was the son of this Pastor who was in Zorzor. Therefore, by noon, the Guinean military, which had a good relationship with the rebels, arrived in rebels-controlled Zorzor to verify the story.

It did not take them long to find Prophet Tamba Bonkay, a famous man of God in the city. He and all those with him, including Esther, brought my father to Guinea in a military convoy to confirm I was his son and to also look after me. This fulfilled the prophetic revelation brought by Esther on that day. Indeed, God is so good as one miracle led to another as they, too, were praying to flee the war zone. And here, they were escorted to safety by the Guinean military.

WOUNDS CURED THROUGH DREAM

While I was in the clinic under medical care, it reached the point that the sores from my wounds weren't healing as expected, and I began to pray for God's healing of my sores because that wasn't good news for me. I remember there was a Liberian fellow who was also brought to that clinic whose ear was removed by rebels, and he died of tetanus in a short period of time. Nevertheless, here I was, alive, with all those wounds on my body not curing in a remote Guinean clinic. So, one night I had a visitor in my dream, a Pastor who was part of the denomination to which we belonged. He was a friend of my spiritual father who came into my hospital room. He didn't say a word, but straightaway removed all the bandages and plasters that were covering my wounds. When I looked, I saw in his hands a container of white powder. He poured the powder on all the wounds on my body, and after he did that, he restored the bandages, and then he promptly disappeared without saying a word. I must report to you that it did not take long after that before all those sores were cured.

WONDER OF MY FIRST OVERSEAS TRIP

Many years ago, life was hard for me and my family as I struggled to finish college while taking care of my wife and three children. At that time, we had no constant form of income. We lived solely by faith as we led a small church in Congo Town. I remember that at that time, a colleague I worked with in the ministry was invited to travel to the US with some delegates to attend a conference. He asked me to join him on the trip. The fact that my dad lives in the US and is established there, and because life was tough on us, would have made it very interesting and natural to jump on board to make the trip.

However, it will interest you to know that I turned it down and conceded the opportunity to a sister who really wanted to travel to the US and who worked along with me as a leader in our small church. The truth is that that year, almost all those who took advantage of that trip got their visas and traveled to the US. And because of the economic situation in the country at the time when we had just come from war, none of them returned. I would have been in the same category had I gone.

Seven years later, I was out of Bible college, and we had planted two churches and a small school operating in our makeshift church building. I decided to go to the US and establish partnerships to enhance the ministry's work. By then, I had a US missionary friend, Brendon Shank, in Liberia who was very helpful to my family and ministry. One day, I asked him to teach me how to fish; don't give me a fish. By this, I meant that while I appreciated his enormous support, I wanted him to help me get to the US, so I could build alliances that would help expand our ministries. Brendon welcomed the idea and promised to help me get an invitation that would allow me to get a visa for the US.

Meanwhile, it didn't take long, and he secured an invitation for me through his parents' church, Broadfording Bible Brethren Church, in Maryland, USA. However, before the invitation arrived in Liberia, I had a dream, and in my dream, I saw myself at the US embassy for an interview. At the interview, I presented my documents and was denied the visa. After the denial, I was disheartened and started walking out of the embassy. But suddenly, the counselor who interviewed me suddenly called me back. When I approached the counter where she was, she presented me with the visa, and, of course, I was elated as I walked out, and then I woke up.

Therefore, after the arrival of the invitation letter, I promptly booked an appointment for a visa interview. When the day came for my appointment, my interviewer or counselor was the lady I had seen in the dream, and like the dream, she easily denied me a visa because of my poor travel history and economic standing, I assume. I left the embassy very disappointed but not very surprised because I saw it coming as revealed by God. However, I knew within myself that it was not over. Sometimes, "it is not over until God says it is over." I felt that "that setback was just a setup for a greater comeback".

Meanwhile, in those days, the visa policy was that when one was refused a visa, he or she would have to wait for 6 months to reapply. Here, I was reminded of the revelation God gave me, that I would go back and get the visa. The next morning, I took off to see my friend Brendon, and I gave him the rundown of what had happened at the embassy. However, told him I had plans to go back and appeal the decision even though the refusal letter said, "decision made today cannot be appealed." That's how powerful US visa counselors are, but the heart of kings is in the hands of God, and He can turn it wherever he chooses. *"In the Lord's hand, the king's heart is a stream of water that he channels toward all who please him"* (Proverbs 21:1 NIV).

That same day, I told Brendon I wanted him to take me back to the embassy since I had no appointment. As an American, I said that he could help appeal on my behalf. My friend Brendon, a quiet and introverted person, found it very difficult to accept to do so, but after nagging and pushing, he finally decided to go with me to give it a trial. It will interest you to know that after Brendon returned my passport and documents to the same counselor with an appeal, she overturned her own decision and promised to grant me the visa.

It did not take long before he came out of the embassy to where I was out waiting for him. He shouted, "David, I have good news for you! Your visa will be granted." Hallelujah! Protocols were broken, a powerful decision overturned, and the wonders of prophetic revelation were manifested.

SIX MONTHS WONDER BUILDING

In 2020, during the heat of the COVID-19 crisis, when most of the world was shut down because of COVID-19's effect, God was doing wonders, and we can testify of God's wonders during this period. While we had a few weeks of lockdown of worship facilities, most churches in Liberia were almost fully operational during this critical period.

We embarked on our annual 21-day fast and prayer in September of that year. As we entered the last week of the fast and prayer, we started a prayer revival, which resulted in a massive outpouring of the power of God and brought many people. Every night, an overflow caused people to be on the church's porch and in the yard. At that point, I was enormously impressed that God was making a big statement to us that it was necessary to construct a bigger building. At that juncture, before the end of the revival, I declared that the following year, there would be a new and larger building capable of receiving everyone who came to our church services.

Meanwhile, at the end of that period of fasting and prayer, I had a dream that night. I saw a friend of mine, a faithful ministry partner, who I had tried calling to give some ministry updates before the night of the dream but could not reach him on the phone. In my dream, he pointed to the beautiful, elevated church building, and excitedly, I woke up. When I woke up, I told my wife I had a lovely dream during the night about the church, and I saw someone in my dream, so I knew that I had to call him. Unlike my other attempts to communicate with him, he answered the call as soon as the phone rang. I immediately began with my updates, especially with the excitement of the growth we saw during that period and the need for a more prominent building. When I mentioned the need for a bigger building, he asked if we had a plan for the building, including an estimate. I said no, but we could assemble and submit a plan later.

Just as it happened in my dream, that phone call conversation was the beginning of a fast-tracked miracle: the building was worth nearly 150,000 USD in six months at a time when the economies of the world were shattered. After presenting the blueprint of the building, the Lord opened a supernatural door in a few months, and we got a commitment for 100 percent financial support. As the work commenced, we soon realized that we needed more than double the amount previously estimated due to the inflation and high cost of building materials and additional needful compartments attached to the building.

Despite the troubled economy and budgetary changes, we did not run out of materials or cash until the work was completed in six months. God was providing from everywhere, both abroad and locally. At the end of the project, our builders confessed to me that in all their careers, they had never worked on any project that was so fast and kept working until it was complete. God is so good.

Toward the end of 2022, we had a situation where all our two vehicles, the church missions' car, and our private car engines, got permanently damaged. This happened around the same time. As a result, our movements were restricted as we mostly traveled through our poor public transportation system. This situation caused immense inconveniences and the inability to achieve daily ministerial goals fully. Since we are involved with numerous ministry projects, prioritizing the purchase of a new car was off our table. However, one night in my dream, someone brought me a black SUV on a long truck and delivered it as a gift. You can imagine how happy I was. However, I was incredibly disillusioned when I woke up from my sleep and realized it was a dream.

Meanwhile, months later, I decided to buy a well-used engine for one of the vehicles, hoping to help us move from point A to point B. After purchasing the engine and installing it in the vehicle, we realized it was defective and hurriedly returned it to the seller. They gave us another one, which was worse than the first one. To add insult to injury, my money wasn't returned to me right away as it was supposed to be to enable me to go elsewhere and get another engine.

After many frustrations and harrowing ordeals, I could still not recuperate my money. So, one morning, I returned to the shop where I had bought the engine and got angry. As I was expressing profound displeasure, the owner of the store, a Liberian who resides in South Korea but owns used car businesses in Liberia, was on a call to the shop and heard me in the background voicing my frustration. He asked his shop manager to give me the phone as he wanted to talk to me. When I got on the phone, he pleaded with me to calm down and assured me I would get my refund. Not only that, but he also told me that he would get me a new car in apology for my troubles. How that new car thing came from his mouth had to be God.

As a result, a few months later, this store owner and used car dealer, a Muslim I had never met before, delivered the black SUV I saw in my dream to my house. This happened while I was in Conakry, Guinea, doing mission work. How great is our God!

MORE VISA WONDERS

After four years of being grounded home without any foreign travel largely due to COVID-19 travel restrictions, at the beginning of 2023, doors began to open for travel. For a few years during the pandemic, like many other embassies, the US embassy remained closed to the public for visa processing except for emergencies. We had missed our twin daughters' graduation from high school in the USA as we could not get a visa interview appointment.

Finally, towards the end of 2022, the US embassy granted me a visa appointment for January 2023 after being in the cue for a while. However, I had a trip to Zambia to attend a marketplace apostolic training that same month, a trip I couldn't afford to miss being Liberia's Country Director, as I had already missed a few CBMC trips. The African director told me they would have been very disappointed had I missed the trip and would also not have had the opportunity to start CBMC in other African countries, as that was the main purpose of the Zambia trip.

Meanwhile, on the eve of my Zambia trip, I was supposed to do my US visa interview, which meant if approved, my passport would have stayed in the embassy for a few days, probably a week. I remember talking to Alex Chisanga, the CBMC Africa Director, about my complicated situation and mentioned that I would likely miss the Zambia training. He warned me of how disappointed they would be. He also spoke of losing the chance to pioneer CBMC, especially in the West African region, which I yearned to do as an Apostle.

So, one night, weeks before my interview, I had a dream. In my dream, I was at the US embassy compound for my visa interview when suddenly, the lights went off completely. I looked for a way to put the lights back on, but all to no avail until I woke up. When I woke up, I knew a US visa problem had been looming since 2007, when I had my only denial, but I bounced back in a few days, just as the prophetic revelation depicted.

On the day of my interview, I planned to ask the counselor to fast-track my visa once approved, enabling me to travel to Zambia in two days. However, I was denied the visa for the first time in 16 years. Just as the dream depicted darkness in the embassy, the Lord shut that door to allow me to go to Zambia, as I needed to leave two days later. Even though I was refused the visa, it was a relief for me because how in the world would I have convinced a difficult counselor to fast-track my visa even if he had approved it? It was almost an impossible venture, so the Lord closed that door, and for the next two days, I was on the plane to Zambia. I had a lifetime experience in Zambia I will never forget.

A few months later, I embarked on another journey to speak at a church conference in Wales, the United Kingdom. I needed to go to neighboring Sierra Leone to apply for my visa, as the UK embassy in Liberia doesn't issue visas. On this one, I was concerned about the possibility of having a challenge with my visa approval even though I had been to the UK on multiple occasions because the UK and the US share visa information; nevertheless, I went to Sierra Leone and submitted my visa application.

After my application, one week later, while uncertain about the outcome, I had a dream on Saturday night; in my dream, I was wearing new white sneakers, and moreover, I saw myself traveling. The next day was Sunday. My wife and Hawa, our church administrator, were together, and I remember sharing with them the dream. I told them my visa would be approved tomorrow, which was Monday, and they joked about saying, "How sure are you?" The following Monday, I received an email from the UK embassy in Sierra Leone stating that my visa had been approved. A few hours later, the same day, I got another email that my passport was coming via DHL. Yes, the Lord is good.

REVELATIONAL WONDER OF GRANDMA GOING TO GLORY

One of the outstanding revelational wonders that I have experienced over the years is the ability to get a signal in the spirit when the death of a close relative, church member, or community member is about to occur. I remembered a few years before the death of my dearest mother-in-law, and in my dream; we were planning her funeral. I woke up and told my wife, and it wasn't long after that when she passed away.

Meanwhile, in October 2022, I lost my dearest grandmother, who meant a lot to me. She was responsible for my upbringing. She was my father's mother, and she took custody of me when I was a toddler. She was everything to me as far as my upbringing is concerned. My grandma was blessed with many years as she was arguably the oldest Kissi woman in Foya district before her passing. As she was stricken by age, on many occasions family members with her would predict she would not live to see the next day as there was so much uncertainty about when she would finally go home to be with the Lord. One night, I had a dream, and in my dream, I had a perfume bottle in my hands, and suddenly, the bottle fell from my hands and broke into pieces. I foolishly decided to collect the broken pieces of bottles and the wasted perfume, but all to no avail. Then I woke up.

I remember telling my wife the dream and unknowingly making a prophetic declaration as I said to her, I have a strong feeling that grandma will go home today. It was two hours later I got a call from my hometown informing me that she had passed away early that morning, about the same time that I had the dream when she was saying goodbye. The wonders of prophetic revelation.

Let me pray for you now.

Heavenly Father, I pray for the reader of this revelational testimony that you will open his or her eyes, and they will have the ability to see pending crises in their personal lives, the family, and the community in the mighty name of Jesus. Amen!

REVELATIONS ON RESULTS OF PRESIDENTIAL ELECTIONS

As I conclude this chapter on revelational wonders, I would like to present to you an encounter I had with the Lord on two separate occasions. These encounters shifted the trajectory of nations and ushered in new governments.

As I delve into this portion, I would like to make a disclaimer, that while this session of my book is politically sensitive, these are direct revelations I received from my Heavenly Father, which came to pass 100 percent as revealed to me by God, and they have nothing to do with my political persuasions. As a matter of fact, I am not a member of any political party, nor do I by any means at home and abroad promote the political agenda of any politician. One thing I know for sure is that I belong to God's party and vote for politicians whose personal character and political persecutions are aligned with biblical standards.

To begin with, I will share with you my dream of the 2020 US presidential elections, which were actually in the embryonic stages of campaigning during the primaries. Both the Republican Party of former President Donald Trump and the Democratic Party of current President Joe Biden were locked down in the primary battles for who would represent their respective parties in the 2020 presidential elections.

One night in my dream the Lord took me to the White House. The truth is that I have been at the White House just once, and that was in 2019 during my last US visit. It was not an official visit, but outside the White House fence where tourists usually go to get a glance of the Presidential Residence, which is considered the most powerful office in the world. In my dream, I was in the White House where the Lord had taken me for a reason; to reveal to me, upfront, the results of the US presidential elections.

As I entered the White House, I saw President Trump seated in the presidential chair and I drew closer to him. I realized that he was angry at me. The closer I drew to him, the angrier he became. Suddenly, I saw him melting from the chair! I mean, his body, the clothes, and everything turned into liquid, and he melted away completely! Immediately, I woke up from sleep, and as the day broke, I told my wife, who is usually the first recipient of my prophetic dreams. I remember saying to her and the few people to whom I recounted this dream that President Trump would lose the election.

Meanwhile, to confirm this, I had another dream, and this time, it was President Joe Biden and his wife, Dr. Jill Biden, visiting Liberia. In my dream, I was president, and my wife was the first lady. Veronica and I formally invited the Bidens to Liberia, and we were giving them a tour of key places in Monrovia. As we were showing them around the city, I woke up, and then I told people that regardless of what happened, Biden would win the US elections that year.

A few months later, the US elections were conducted, and President Joe Biden was declared the winner. What an outstanding turnout. While we are revealing these revelational wonders, I would like to categorically do a disclaimer that these revelations do not in any way project that God had a favorite person anointed as the winner, but the truth is that in these uncertain seasons, God chooses to reveal to his servants upfront how these elections turn out. And this is a clear demonstration of his wonders among his people. Furthermore, bringing into fulfillment the Word of the Lord, which says, *"And he said, Hear now my words: If there be a prophet among you, I the LORD will make myself known unto him in a vision, and will speak unto him in a dream."* (Numbers 12:6, KJV).

WONDER OF THE 2023 LIBERIA'S PRESIDENTIAL ELECTIONS

Recently, our nation, Liberia, just concluded legislative and presidential elections. It was an election that was crucial to the sustainability of the peace of the nation because this was the first post-war presidential election independently run by the Liberian government without the involvement of the international community, especially from a security standpoint. As the elections drew near, people were worried about the outcome because the incumbent was facing a serious challenge as the opposition in preceding legislative elections turned out to be stronger than the ruling establishment. Moreover, it is believed that it is almost impossible for an incumbent to lose an election in Africa as they are most likely to complete their final term using whatever means available to them to accomplish their wish.

Meanwhile, it was during this crucial period of uncertainty that the Lord revealed to me in advance what would be the outcome of the elections, and that began with the vision for national shifting that was coming, which led to the writing and released of my latest book, *A Prophetic Call for National Shifting*. The book was launched in September 2023, a week before the election, which was held on October 10. The results of the October 10 elections showed a virtual tie between the incumbent president, George Weah, and his main challenger, opposition leader, former Vice President Joseph Boakai, as they both finished with 43 percent each, and the other parties shared the rest of the votes.

As a result, the first round of votes saw no presidential candidate getting the needed 50 percent plus 1 vote to avoid a runoff. Therefore, a runoff election was declared by the National Elections Commission, which was scheduled for November 14. Consequently, a couple of weeks before the runoff, the Lord revealed to me in the dream that former Vice President Joseph Boakai would narrowly win the elections.

So, one night in my dream, I was in a car with the now-president-elect Joe Boakai. He was driving, and I sat in the back and watched as he drove. We arrived at a gate heavily manned by military men as we drove. It was difficult to gain access, but the driver, the president-elect, exited the car and conversed with those manning the fortified gate. He was allowed passage, and we passed through the gate when it opened.

As we went further on this trip, we again arrived at another gate; this time, it was even more fortified and manned than the last one, and just like the first one, he descended the vehicle; after the conversation, we were allowed to pass. As I sat in the passenger seat, I watched us pass through all these gates and then came the third and final gate, which was once again fortified than all the others. like the previous gates, he descended the vehicle, and after the conversation, our vehicle was allowed to pass through that gate. As we passed the third and final gate, I immediately woke up from my sleep and told my wife that morning that Joseph Boakai was set to win the election. I told her, and those close to me, that it would be tough and tight, but he would emerge victorious.

Meanwhile, we can announce that, by God's divine revelation, Joseph Nyuma Boakai narrowly defeated the incumbent president, George Weah, in the runoff. He will be inaugurated as the 25th president of Liberia on January 22nd, 2024. So, to God be the glory.

CHAPTER FOUR

THE WONDERS OF GOD'S PROTECTION

Over the last 30 years of my life, I have seen the protective hand of God at work greatly, and had it not been for the Lord's protection, I would have exited this planet in 2003 at the age of 17. But God showed himself strong and my life was spared.

The Prophet Isaiah declares these words of God.

But now thus says the LORD, he who created you, O Jacob, he who formed you, O Israel: "Fear not, for I have redeemed you; I have called you by name, you are mine. When you pass through the waters, I will be with you; and through the rivers, they shall not overwhelm you; when you walk through fire you shall not be burned, and the flame shall not consume you. For I am the LORD your God, the Holy One of Israel, your Savior. I give Egypt as your ransom, Cush and Seba in exchange for you. (Isaiah 43:1-3, ESV)

Among the thousands of God's promises, this is one of my favorites, for I have experienced this promise in a massive way over the years.

FAILURE OF THE MACHETE AND THE MACHINE GUNS

So, in 2003, two years after surrendering my life to Christ, I began serving as a lay minister of the Gospel alongside my deceased spiritual father, who led me to Christ. It was during this time that I experienced a protective miracle that changed my life forever.

We had moved from Gbarnga Bong County, where I surrendered my life to Christ. It was there that my spiritual father, Tamba Bongay, ran a small church. However, in 2001, his denomination assigned him to pastor a church in Zorzor Lofa County. Therefore, we moved to Zorzor Lofa County to take on the new assignment, and there, I served as an assistant minister to my spiritual father.

Nearly two years into the Lofa ministry, all hell broke loose on February 11, 2003, as rebels of the ULIMO attacked Zorzor to remove the NPFL rebels led by former rebel leader and president Charles Taylor from the city. It was not a good day as my spiritual father had gone to the hospital to get some medical attention. As a result of the heavy fighting that was going on in the city, few of the church members ran to the church compound for refuge and there they decided to flee the city to seek refuge in a nearby village. In the absence of my spiritual father, I led the group of members to the village to seek refuge.

A few weeks later, in March of that year, rebels of the NPFL passed through our refuge village one night and decided to launch an attack on their opponents in the city to retake it. When they arrived in our village, they came with a preconceived mindset that there were ULIMO rebels in that village. Therefore, without any mercy whatsoever, decided to slaughter the inhabitants of the village, especially men who were beaten and beheaded when seen.

As they asked everyone to leave their houses to come out, I refused to obey their orders but prostrated myself and began to cry out to God in prayers for a way out. After praying for a while, the Lord said to me, "Arise and go out; no matter what happens tonight, you will come out alive." With that assurance, I stood up with my faith, elevated, believing in God's protection, and stepped out of the house.

When they saw me, they immediately grabbed me and began beating and stabbing me from the back and eventually laid me down to behead me as they had done to the other men before me.

In the process of beheading me, something miraculous happened in the twinkling of an eye. My would-be killers were frozen as the man who was cutting off my head stopped, and so those who were holding me stopped as well. Meanwhile, I also realized that the ropes that I was tied with went loose, and at that juncture, I noticed that deliverance had come. A miracle was in the making, and the wonders of God's protection were in full display.

Therefore, having realized that I was freed, I rose and began running for my life. After a few seconds, I realized we were back at square one as the rebels got on the chase to finish me up and the next thing I heard was the sound of machine guns from my back at a very close range. I remember that night there was moonlight, and it would have been easy to shoot me. However, as the shooting was going on, I felt a massive wind from my backside that threw me on the ground. When I fell, the rebels thought they had hit their target, and they stopped and returned to the village.

Meanwhile, despite all that I had already been through with

the machete and guns, I was still alive, lying there in the blood pouring from the wounded parts of my body. After a few minutes when I realized the rebels were no longer in sight. I stood, and at this point, I wasn't sure if I was on earth or somewhere in paradise. I began to test my senses and feel things around me, and when I placed my hands on my neck, I felt a deep wound from the machete with a lot of blood coming out. Yet, during all I went through, the Lord protected me.

The next day, the Lord guided me to Guinea, which was a miracle to have traveled to another country with all the wounds, with no human assistance. When I arrived in Guinea at a clinic in Koinyama, it was confirmed by Doctor Mansor that no bullet had touched me. To God be the glory.

THE 9/11 ATTACK

On September 1, 2003, my family and I experienced yet another display of the protective hands of the almighty God. Usually, in Liberia and West Africa, this is a period of occasional but heavy downpours of rain, and every so often they are accompanied by thunderstorms. In the early morning hours of September 1st, we were all up; my wife Veronica and our twin daughters, who shared our bedroom with us at the time. We could not come out of the house because it was raining torrentially.

While in the room lying on the bed, my daughters were on me wrestling, and suddenly, the lightning struck, and our room was under attack in the twinkling of an eye. I noticed my daughters were off me because I was the target of the attack. At this juncture, I was in a near-death situation and didn't know what was happening. Later, my wife told me that all she saw was fire hovering over me, but it couldn't touch me. Then, it suddenly vanished. But not without destroying the power generator as well a CD player that we had in the house.

When I came to, I literally jumped out of the room and began praising God in the community while it was still raining. Our neighbors were all concerned if anything had happened to any of us because they knew that the lightning that struck landed in the community. They were amazed that we all came out alive, save the power generator and CD player. *"No weapon forged against you will prevail, and you will refute every tongue that accuses you. This is the heritage of the servants of the Lord, and this is their vindication from me," declares the Lord.* (Isaiah 54:17 NIV).

Certainly, the protection of the almighty God is an inherent right of those who believe in the Lord and have become his sons and daughters. Give your life to Christ today, and you will begin to enjoy this right.

As I conclude this testimony on God's protective power, please allow me to pray for you as you go through difficult and defining moments of your life that demand heavenly cover for your survival and well-being.

Heavenly Father, I pray that the one reading this testimony will experience their share of your ever-potent and powerful hand of protection in the midst of their storms, difficult moments, and defining moments of their lives. May every bullet and arrow released by the enemy against them be neutralized in the mighty name of Jesus! May every plan to attack, to cause harm, be nullified from its very inception in the mighty name of Jesus!

CHAPTER FIVE

SUPERNATURAL PROVISION

"But my God shall supply all your needs according to his riches in glory by Christ Jesus."

PHILIPPIANS 4:19 KJV

I n this chapter, we will dwell on how God provides for the needs of his children in ways that are sometimes unimaginable. When the going gets tough, the road gets rocky and bumpy, and there is no way to proceed after exerting all human efforts; that's when God shows up at times mightily.

in the previous chapter, we discussed revelational wonders. It's important to note that revelation is not a complete wonder without its physical realistic aspects. A dream remains a dream, and a vision remains a vision, but when it is brought to fruition through physical and realistic means, it becomes a wonder. The revelational testimonies shared in the previous chapter were made possible only because of the physical manifestations of prophetic dreams.

THE ELEVENTH-HOUR GOD

Our God is the God of the eleventh hour. I have seen Him step in at times when mankind has lost it, given up, and been in hopeless and helpless situations. Every so often, God allows us to go through extremely difficult times, and when you think it is all over, boom, He shows. This is true of occurrences in biblical history in both the Old and New Testaments.

There was a time in the life of the Jews in Exile when they were about to be extinguished completely because of the wicked plots of Haman. In Esther chapter three, it is reported that Haman, who was elevated in the kingdom of Persia and a close associate of the King, plotted to destroy the Jews only because Mordecai the Jew refused to bow to him as did the others in the king palace every morning as he passed by. The plot was well on the way, King Ahasuerus had bought into the wicked scheme, the deal was signed, and the date was set that the Jews be destroyed.

Meanwhile, at the eleventh hour, it took a faithful Mordecai to provoke Esther the Queen to invoke the intervention of the 11th-hour God:

For if you remain silent at this time, relief and deliverance for the Jews will arise from another place, but you and your father's family will perish. And who knows but that you have come to your royal position for such a time as this?" Then Esther sent this reply to Mordecai: "Go, gather together all the Jews who are in Susa, and fast for me. Do not eat or drink for three days, night or day. I and my attendants will fast as you do. When this is done, I will go to the king, even though it is against the law. And if I perish, I perish.

ESTHER 4:14-16 NIV

These passages of Scripture clearly indicate Queen Esther being provoked by her uncle Mordecai to rise to the occasion at the eleventh hour of what would have been the annihilation of the Jewish people in exile. Esther responds positively by declaring a three-day fast and prayer for her and her attendants and the entire Jewish community. In chapter five, on the third and last day of fasting and prayer, Esther shows up at the King's palace. This was a scenario that was totally unlawful and could have cost her life, but she foregoes her personal well-being and trusts in God. As a result, she found favor in the king's eyes, and there was deliverance for the Jewish people. That wicked man, Haman was hanged on the very gallows he had prepared for Mordecai, and the Jews were saved.

Many years ago, at the age of seventeen, my life was about to be taken in a gruesome way; by beheading. Other men and young boys in my village had already been severely beaten and beheaded by rebels who had surrounded our village of refuge during our civil war in Liberia. As I stepped out of my village house, after praying to God for his intervention in the eleventh hour, and God showed up for me. As I came out, I realized all the young men who had hastily stepped out before me at the demand of the rebels were already executed by beheading, and it was my turn to be killed.

I was stabbed in the back many times, and quickly, I found myself lying down to be beheaded like those before me. At this crucial juncture, I needed the intervention of the God of the eleventh hour. Remember, in my earlier chapter, I mentioned Esther and my spiritual father, who were fasting and praying for me, and those with me in the village and had the dream that showed me returning with a palm branch in my hands. Truly, the God of the eleventh hour is real, and he did it for me. At the point of being decapitated, He stepped in, confounded my would-be killers, and found a way of escape for me.

> One day, Jesus and His disciples were out on the lake in a boat, and as they crossed the lake to get to the other side, Jesus fell asleep. During that time, a great storm arose, and they were in grave danger, as the boat was filling with water and in danger of capsizing because of the enormous storm. However, Jesus was fast asleep in the boat, and they woke him up. "And they went and woke him, saying, "Master, Master, we are perishing!" And he awoke and rebuked the wind and the raging waves, and they ceased, and there was a calm."
>
> LUKE 8:23-24 NIV

It is not that Jesus didn't know there was a storm ahead. In fact, being God, He knew exactly what was ahead of them. Yet ironically, he was fast asleep when all this was happening. I believe he was allowing the situation to get to the eleventh hour and then stepping in as He usually does. That was precisely what He did; he stepped in, and calm was restored.

Many years ago, when the Lord delivered me from the machete and guns and led me to Guinea for safety. A Guinean family found me severely wounded and wandering in the bush. Seeing my perilous condition, they felt that they had no alternative but to get me to the town and take me before the military authority. The very fact that I even arrived in that country, considering the grave extent of my injuries and physical condition, can only be attributed to the supernatural intervention of God.

When they brought me to the military authority, I was inter-rogated a bit. Miraculously, I found favor with a military officer they referred to as, Commando. He had a reputation for dealing ruthlessly with people he perceived as fighters fleeing the war in Liberia. There were instances in which some Liberian men lost their lives at the border during those days when they were per-ceived to be rebels. Yet here I was with blood all over me. It would have been easy to have concluded that I was a wounded fighter fleeing for my life.

But, instead of being killed, I found favor with Commando, who then, briefly interrogated me. I was at that eleventh hour of survival. I say the eleventh hour because, by this time, I was losing my ability to speak, and was unable even to eat. Imagine I was now into the second night of my horrible ordeal without adequate medical attention. This was an extreme emergency. Nevertheless, God intervened and found a way to take me to safety, where I could receive the vital medical attention I so desperately needed.

So, Commando went into the town, hastily mobilized young men, and got a hammock to put me in. Back then (and this is still happening in isolated villages and towns where there are no means of modern transportation), the sick or those needing urgent medical care were transported to a nearby village or town where there was a clinic in a hammock.

Commando literally ran ahead in every village we were ap-proaching to recruit fresh strength to continue the journey. Commando was restless until I was delivered to the clinic in Koinyama, where I received life-saving medical treatment. My God is truly the God of the eleventh hour.

As I conclude this chapter, I would like to encourage the person who is about to give up. You feel that you have done everything to the best of your knowledge and ability, but the results are the same. In fact, it's getting worse. You have reached a breaking point, a point of surrendering and throwing in the towel. I have been here before. Many others have also been in your position as well. Yet, we have seen the hand of God in supernatural displays, changing stories, breaking barriers, removing mountains, opening new chapters, and changing lives at the eleventh hour. You are next in line. Your miracle is on the way. Your story is about to change. All I ask of you is to stand still and see the salvation of God, as did the Israelis at the Red Sea.

While on their escape journey from the bondage and slavery in Egypt, God supernaturally provided a way of escape at the eleventh hour when they had gotten stuck at the Red Sea, and their enemies, the Egyptians were fast approaching.

Since, therefore, the children share in flesh and blood, he himself likewise partook of the same things, that through death he might destroy the one who has the power of death, that is, the devil, and deliver all those who through fear of death were subject to lifelong slavery.

HEBREWS 2:14-15, ESV

They began to complain and murmur that it was better to stay and die in Egypt and have graves, but there they were about to die in the desert without graves. At that desperate juncture, Moses had to call them to order.

And Moses said unto the people, Fear ye not, stand still, and see the salvation of the LORD, which he will shew to you today: for the Egyptians whom ye have seen today, ye shall see them again no more forever. The LORD shall fight for you, and ye shall hold your peace.

EXODUS 14:13-14, KJV

Here we see a desperate people who are on the verge of being destroyed in the desert by their enemies, the Egyptians. As they looked behind them, they saw the enemy in sight and fast approaching, and as they looked before them, all they saw was the massive Red Sea, and they were ready to give up. But God called them to order through His servant Moses because He was about to provide a miraculous way of escape and destroy their enemies once and for all. The rest of this story is a perfect example of the move of God in the eleventh hour of turbulent times.

First, the Lord placed darkness between the fast-approaching Egyptians and Israel so they could not approach them even though they were so close. He also caused the Red Sea to split, thereby creating massive walls on both sides, and dry land appeared. The people of Israel walked through the midst of the Red Sea on dry land until they crossed over to the other side. Finally, Pharaoh and his army tried to follow them but were all destroyed as they drowned in the Red Sea because God closed the waters of the sea behind the people of Israel. We can see that the key to this move of God is the ability to stand still and keep the faith during turbulent times.

It is my prayer that regardless of what you are going through today, you would trust and be still; that you would keep the faith, and that you would look to God in your turbulent times. Like David said, *"I will lift my eyes unto the hills, from whence cometh my help. My help cometh from the LORD, which made heaven and earth."* (Psalms 121:1-2, KJV)" By this, you will certainly, without a shadow of doubt, see the hand of God at work in that situation. AMEN!

CHAPTER SIX

HEALING WONDERS

"He sent out his word and healed them and delivered them from their destruction."

PSALMS 107:20, ESV

F rom the day Adam and Eve fell in the garden, the body of man became corruptible and subject to all kinds of destructive diseases and calamities that have ravished the creatures of God on earth in all manner of ways. However, God has put into place plans to mitigate this situation by providing healing for those who believe in him.

In this chapter, we shall endeavor to highlight the healing miracles orchestrated by our Lord and Savior, Jesus Christ. Over the years, I have seen the hand of God at work in my life and in the lives of many, healing all manner of sicknesses and situations for his glory.

My first encounter with a healing miracle was my calling experience. In the early 90s, while I was in the streets in Gbarnga Bong County, the then Charles Taylor's rebel headquarters, living a riotous and rebellious life, suddenly, I began to experience insanity. I couldn't comprehend what was happening to me, and my friends around me were also confused and couldn't figure out what to do with me as I was far away from my family.

Meanwhile, one of them suggested that the best thing to have done for me was to take me to a well-known Prophet, Tamba Bongay, who was in the city known for his prophetic gifting and healing ministry. It was there and then that I experienced, first, the greatest of all miracles, which is salvation, as I surrendered my life to Christ and received him as savior and Lord. The next miracle was the healing miracle as my insanity was gone, and I became very normal. it was then that I felt the call of God upon my life and chose never to turn my back on God. God is so good.

THE HEALING VISITOR

In continuation of my miraculous survival story, I was brought to the clinic in Koinyama by Commando and the men he recruited along the way from village to village. I was notified by the nurse who was responsible for cleaning my wounds, that after going through treatment, it became evident that they were not getting better.

Meanwhile, at that juncture, I went to God in prayer and pleaded with my Heavenly Father for my complete healing. Then, one night, I had a dream, and in my dream, a pastor who was part of my church denomination who had visited us once before the attack came into my hospital room. When he entered, he didn't say anything but immediately began to remove the bandages I had around my neck and, on my back, where I had sustained horrible wounds and severe injuries during the attack. After removing everything, a small bottle of white powder appeared in his hands. He then poured that power on every affected area of my body. After that procedure, he re-bandaged all the wounds, and then, he disappeared.

Praise God! That dream marked the beginning of my healing journey at the clinic, and it did not take long for the narrative to change as my sores were curing, and I walked out of the clinic totally healed! As a matter of counting my blessings, I still remember there was a fellow Liberian who was also brought to that same Guinean clinic who had one ear cut off by rebels across the border. Sadly, he didn't survive his injury to tell the story, as he died from tetanus due to the poor conditions of the health facility during those days. Meanwhile, I can count my blessings and attribute my healing and survival to the almighty God whose intervention was pivotal to my recovery. To God, be the glory!

"SILVER AND GOLD HAVE I NONE, BUT SUCH I HAVE GIVE I THEE"

In my preceding healing encounter, I narrated what I consider one of my first recorded healing experiences. As I continue in this chapter, I want to narrate what is the most recent of the many healing miracles I have seen in my personal life and ministry. I call this *"Silver and gold have I none, but such I have give I thee."* This is a quote from Acts 3:1-9 which speaks to Peter and John's experience when on their way to the Temple for prayer in the city of Jerusalem.

The Bible reveals that on their way for prayer to the Temple, they encountered a certain man who was born crippled and sat daily in the open on the way leading into the temple and begged for money from those who went in and out of the Temple daily. It happened that, one day, this handicapped man asked Peter and John for alms he asked of all those who passed by him daily. But, that day, Peter and John gave him a different response altogether. It was a response that changed his life forever.

Instead of giving him money as usual, Peter responded in a singular fashion:

> *And Peter, fastening his eyes upon him with John, said, Look on us. And he gave heed unto them, expecting to receive something of them. Then Peter said, Silver and gold have I none; but such as I have, give I thee: In the name of Jesus Christ of Nazareth, rise up and walk. And he took him by the right hand and lifted him up: and immediately his feet and ankle bones received strength. And he, leaping up, stood, and walked, and entered with them into the temple, walking, and leaping, and praising God.*
>
> ACTS 3:4-8, KJV

The man who was born lame and begged throughout his life due to his disability, got the shock of his life as he received an unexpected healing.

Very recently, the wife of one of our pastors in one of our local churches in Monrovia received healing from a serious infirmity that had her health in rapid deterioration. In fact, I had heard of her getting medication from their community clinic, but to no avail, as she continued to decline. She never had the means of pursuing treatment at a bigger and better-equipped hospital.

Nevertheless, one Saturday morning, I got a surprise visit when I entered the church compound, and there she was on the church's front porch! She was waiting for me, but I was rushing late to teach at ELSOM, a Bible school run by our church, which her husband attends. On seeing her, I was shocked. First, because of her condition. She needed to be home, and not here as one of our students. I didn't understand why she was out there that morning. When I greeted and briefly interacted with her, I realized she had come for me to see her worsening condition.

She needed money to help her go to a bigger and better health facility. However, this was unfolding at a time when I was unable to help her financially because my financial state at the time wasn't good at all to intervene financially. At that Juncture, I said to myself, "Silver and gold have I none, but such I have to give I thee." So, after my classes that afternoon, I called a prayer meeting for her as I asked my Bible school director, Pastor Tengbeh, and her husband, Daniel, to join me as I prayed for her healing. So, we prayed a prayer of faith for her healing, and in the end, I prayed over a bottle of water and gave it to her to drink. She drank some and took the rest home. By faith, I told her she would recover.

Praise God because less than a week later, I received a call from them with a testimony of her healing from that infirmity, and her health has never been the same. To God alone be the glory for His miraculous intervention.

HEALINGS AT THE FARM

By the grace of God, our ministry owns and operates a farm in Tubmanburg Bomi County, and I occasionally visit the farm to catch up with activities. During some of these visits, we have seen the hand of God at work in the village that hosts the farm. Occasionally, our farm manager, Zayzay, has asked me to pray for a few individuals who come purposely to the isolated village for healing. In the village, there is a traditional herbalist who performs healing rituals for those who go to the village for healing, and most times they will be there waiting for a long time to be healed. Some may be healed, some may not, and some may not even survive.

On one of our visits to the farm in January 2023, I had some foreign missionaries with me who were in Liberia on a short-term mission trip. We spent a couple of days in Tubmanburg, the city close to the farm, to enable us to have access to the farm, as we were involved with working in the pineapple field for two days.

On the last day of our trip and work on the farm, Zayzay, our farm manager, asked us to pray for a lady who had a paralyzed leg and was struggling to walk freely. While in the palava hut, I asked the lady to step forward to come forward, and I asked her if she believed in Christ as her Lord and Savior. She responded with a resounding, yes! This is an essential question because Bomi County has a predominantly Muslim population. I also asked her if she believed that Jesus could heal her that very day, and she responded yes. At that juncture, I asked the others with me to join me in prayers for her healing. Praise God because, at the end of the prayer, the lady who was partially paralyzed, and struggling to move around was running all over in the palava hut and praising God for her healing. She was healed in the name of Jesus. A few weeks later, she came to Monrovia at our Central church along with Zayzay to testify of the goodness of God. Yes, our God heals!

Still in the village, on another occasion, there was a young woman who was in the village for an abnormal skin disease that causes rashes and sores on the skin. Zayzay had told me about her situation, and she was also in the village waiting for healing. When she came forward for prayers in the palava hut, I noticed that her skin was covered with rashes and white powder, which the herbalist had used on her. I asked her if she believed in the

Lord Jesus Christ and in his healing powers, and she replied, yes. We prayed for her and left. A few days later, Zayzay called to tell me that her skin was smooth and cured, and she was healed.

In confirmation of this healing miracle, recently, I was in Tubmanburg along with some visiting missionaries from the US, and as I was showing them our rubber farm, a young woman shouted, "Pastor, Pastor!" She came to us and said, "Do you remember me?"

Startled, I replied, "No, I don't."

She said, "I am the girl with the skin disease that you prayed for in the village last year, and I am here to let you know that shortly after you left, I was healed!"

We all were awed by the goodness of the Lord. This was truly a wonder in our pathway on that day.

One day, Zayzay himself came from the farm with a hearing problem. However, before coming to town, he had called me on several occasions and complained about fluid coming out of his ears. He was also experiencing hearing loss. He asked for money to go to the clinic for a checkup and treatment, and we did, but all to no avail, as his condition remained the same.

Eventually, Zayzay came to Monrovia to follow up and get better medical care. During this time, we were having prayer and fasting revival services at the church. On the last day of the services, while praying for the sick, Zayzay stepped forward, and we prayed for his healing. According to his testimony, it is interesting that even though his healing was not instant, that night while in bed, there was what he called "an earthquake" in his ears that he calls the move of God. He said that it started at midnight, and when the day broke, Zayzay realized he was healed; his hearing was restored! The fluid that was coming out of his ears ceased. Our farm guy was healed and has never experienced that affliction again.

HAVE YOU PRAYED YET?

Early this year, my wife was on a trip to Ghana to handle some business while I stayed in Liberia, catching up with my usual busy schedule. Suddenly, I began to experience a severe toothache from a tooth that had recently had a filling. All this happened in the spur of the moment on a very hot day. I rushed to the ELWA hospital dental clinic, where I had the work done on my tooth.

When I showed up at the dental clinic, I was checked and told that the best-case scenario for me was to remove that tooth right away. They told me that there was nothing that could be done to stop the pain. I remember years ago when I had the filling put in, the dentist then told me that they were going to fill the cavity, but the next time I experienced a severe problem in that tooth, they would recommend removal. So, this response didn't come as a surprise at all. However, I was determined not to remove my tooth, especially when my wife wasn't around to play baby on. I am the kind of husband who plays baby on my wife a lot when I am not well, and my wife knows me very well for that. The first thing I thought was, my wife isn't here, and I am not sure how my body will react to the extraction because I had never had a tooth extracted before. It was a hot afternoon, and usually, these procedures are better the first thing in the morning before the day heats up.

Meanwhile, I rejected the whole idea of removing the tooth that afternoon, but I asked them to give me a few painkillers, which they did. Just as they predicted, that night was horrible because I could barely close my eyes because of the pain. The painkillers were of no help whatsoever, even though I almost overdosed at one point when the pain continued, non-stop, until midnight. That's when the Holy Spirit spoke to me by saying,

"Have you prayed yet?" I replied, "No." Now, here is a pastor who has seen the hand of God heavily at work in his life on numerous occasions going through a severe toothache, yet has forgotten to pray for healing. I felt guilty when the Holy Spirit reminded me, and I immediately started praying, asking for mercy and instant healing.

After that reminder of the Holy Spirit and prayer at midnight, the pain immediately ceased, and I finally found relief that night. At that Juncture, I slept well until the following day. Let me announce to you that since then, that pain has never returned, even though my dentist said the only remedy to that pain was to remove the tooth. With that, I learned to hear from God more than man. I am not saying don't follow your doctor's advice. God positions Doctors with the knowledge He gave them to help save lives. However, there are times when faith supersedes everything.

About midnight. Paul and Silas were praying and singing hymns to God, and the prisoners were listening to them, and suddenly, there was a great earthquake, so that the foundations of the prison were shaken. And immediately, all the doors were opened, and everyone's bonds were unfastened.

ACTS 16:25-26, ESV

REFUSED TO COME OUT BUT CHOSE TO PRAY

While highlighting the need to prioritize prayer in times of sickness and every other critical circumstances, I would like to share the decision I took in a crucial hour that led to my survival of the massacre at age 17. While this may not speak directly to healing, the effect of my decision to choose prayer over fears and warnings by bloodthirsty rebels was vital to my deliverance from death, which goes beyond a particular healing experience.

On that fateful night in March 1993, when rebels took over our village and demanded that everyone come out and that if you didn't come out, no one could be killed. Many hurried to exit their houses. But, as I mentioned before, many of the men who obeyed were executed almost instantly! They were all decapitated.

Meanwhile, I chose a different approach when even the brother I shared the room with, Elijah, was also killed as he fearfully came out of the house. I decided to lay prostrate myself on the ground and prayed. I asked God to intervene in that critical hour. I prayed my favorite Scripture, Psalm 23, during that time of need. I love verse 4 the most. "*Yea though I walk through the valley of the shadow of death, I will fear no evil: for thou are with me; thy rod and thy staff they comfort me.*" (Psalm 23:4)

Once, I was invited to speak at Jubilee Praise Worship Center, and the bishop told me that he was teaching Psalm 23 in a series of teachings for an entire month. He requested that I teach verse 4, which is my favorite one. I love that verse because I know what a meant for my deliverance that night as I prayed and declared while lying down and praying in that critical hour of facing death. I read that Psalm over and over, and finally, it was time to come out to face my would-be killers. By this time, my faith had jumped when the Lord said to me, "No matter what happens tonight, you will come out alive." Encouraged by this word, I rose and opened the door, and the rest of the story is my supernatural escape simply because I chose prayer over fear and threats.

Even as I write this book, I have experienced a personal healing miracle that came not as a surprise but as a reminder of the need to prioritize prayer whenever faced with an unbearable situation. So, I woke up yesterday morning with a sharp pain on the left side of my heart, so much so that breathing became a bit difficult.

The pain was so intense that I felt that it would be impossible for me to go to the gym for my usual exercise. Even climbing the stairs on the second floor of the church office was painful. Meanwhile, this continued throughout the day but was intermittent with on-and-off pain. So, as I woke up this early morning at my usual wake-up time, either for prayer or to write, I experienced a similar sharp pain in the same area as I entered the bathroom to attend to nature. Instantly, I was reminded of the need to pray, which I had not done.

So, while in the bathroom, I placed my right hand on my chest where the pain was situated, and I spoke to it, saying, "GET OUT, pain, in the name of Jesus!" Praise God! When I finished that short prayer, the pain had obeyed and checked out. I walked out of the bathroom free of pain, and it has never returned. Of course, a miracle is a miracle, and there is no such thing as a small one. Nevertheless, it is vital to apply faith first every time we are faced with an undesirable and unbearable situation.

HEALING OF THE PARALYZED

While we are still on healing wonders, I want to mention a remarkable healing we witnessed during our 21-day annual fast and prayer last year, for it is a testimony worth sharing and applies to this session.

Valerie is one of our teachers at the Excellent Leaders School of Ministries, or ELSOM vocational program. She suddenly fell ill with a strange and sudden illness that nearly led to her death and eventually left her paralyzed.

Valerie was hit in the spur of a moment by what she considers a spiritual attack. She narrates that she was experiencing a very mild cold, and that evening, she passed out. That, she thought, was highly unusual for a mere cold. She further narrates that while unconscious, she found herself in a battle for her life. There was group of individuals trying to take her life, while there was another group fighting to rescue her and restore her to life. During this time, she could see her body lying on the bed as she was floating in the room. As those who fought for her to return to her body and live, her mother and brother performed CPR on her, and her soul and spirit returned to her body.

After returning to her body, she realized that one side of her body was paralyzed, and she lost feelings for that side of the body. She also could not walk at all without help. Since this happened during our 21-day fast and prayer period, she asked to be brought to our church. During our annual fast and prayer, we set up a prayer camp at the church where prayers are made day and night. During this time, we always see God move in a mighty way.

Valerie was brought in helpless as she needed assistance to move from one place to another. Seeing this, we began to pray for her healing and restoration morning and evening. Her healing came progressively as she fully recovered within one week, all in the name of Jesus.

INSTANT HEALING OF SKIN DISEASE

While we are still on healing wonders, I am reminded of the testimony of one of the sisters in our church. Her name is Annie Cooper, and she is in a leadership position for our women's ministries. I caught up with her at church recently and told her about this project, and she was more than happy to share her testimony of God's goodness.

In 2020, she got seriously sick with a skin disease that caused rashes on her skin as well as made her body swollen. She went from hospital to hospital and saw no improvement in her condition or even a diagnosis of probable cause. Meanwhile, she turned to traditional herbal medicine and began to drink boiled leaves and wrapped chalk made from the same leaves as experts had advised for a long period of time. But all to no avail. There were times when it would subside, but then only for a season, but would return with rashes, itching, and swelling.

This went on for a while, and one day, she told herself that she was tired of all this pain and drinking herbal medicine every day with no results. During this time, there was a revival happening at our church, which lasted for several days, and one of the evenings, she stepped forward in faith as I laid hands on the sick and prayed for healing miracles, and something miraculous happened. Praise God that at the end of the prayer for her, she examined her body and realized that the swelling, the rashes on my skin, and the itching were all completely healed! Hallelujah! The incredible thing is that since 2020, she has never experienced a similar illness again. To God be the glory for her healing is complete!

GOD'S REPORT, NOT THE DOCTOR'S REPORT

There are times when we are confronted with a bad report from the doctor after a medical checkup, which has the proclivity to worsen an already existing sickness or situation due to the damaging psychological effect that comes with it. The devil takes advantage of the fear and psychological breakdown one experiences during these crucial times to weaken the defense of individuals in such situations. This worsens their problems and sometimes results in a total breakdown and may lead to premature death. Be careful, for Satan is very crafty.

Here is another beautiful testimony to encourage you. We recently received it from Sister Dorris Williams, a member of our church. This testimony emanates from our recent annual 21-day fast and prayer, which is held in September of every year.

As mentioned, we usually set up a prayer camp at church during this time. This camp is where prayer warriors, especially some of those involved with fasting and prayer, spend all night at the church edifice to participate in the nightly prayers. Moreover, during this time, I, too, am always at the church. We encourage people who aren't fasting but wish to join our early morning prayer service at 6 AM to come and trust God for their healing or whatever problem they have.

Dorris, pregnant at that time, came to the prayers one morning. After prayer, she spoke to my wife regarding a report she received from her doctor about an ultrasound was conducted. In tears, she explained the doctor's report that her child was in the wrong position in her womb, and since she was nearing her delivery period, she had to get prepared for a C-section. My wife brought her forward for prayers, and after explaining her situation, I asked her whose report she would believe: the doctor's report or God's report. She said that she goes with the latter; that is God's report. I told her God's report says you will have a normal delivery, and no knife will touch your body. That was the beginning of her deliverance from C-section.

That morning, we started a prayer for her, specifically asking God to cancel the C-section that the doctor reported and command the child to get back in the right position for a standard delivery. This went on for days as we declared every morning over her. As a result of that effectual and fervent prayer of faith, Dorris recently gave birth through a normal delivery to beautiful twins.

HICCUP CHECKED OUT

While this may seem like an insignificant or small miracle, I am emboldened to share it because of the significant lesson we can learn from it. However, there are no small miracles. A miracle requires the supernatural intervention of God, and therefore, every time God intervenes in a situation, whether small or big, it is a massive deal.

Most recently, I experienced a hiccup, a situation we all experience occasionally, however common it may appear. Hiccups can be a distraction, and I have heard stories of how serious they can be. They can even lead to hospitalization. One night, while in bed, I suddenly began to experience hiccups. They came out of nowhere. I drank water and held my breath, but they continued briefly and then ceased. The next day, almost around the same bedtime, they returned, and this time even more aggressively. I soon realized there was a pattern here, and I needed to stand my ground on God's Word to deal with it.

Meanwhile, after drinking water and holding my breath for a while, this time, they refused to go away. Then, the Holy Spirit reminded me to pray to get rid of it. At that juncture, I declared in the name of Jesus, "I command you hiccups to go, and I mean now!" Praise God! Because at the release of the last of the last word, the hiccups left me instantly and without delay. Our God is incredible!

I am praying for someone who is going through a situation that has become a pattern. I mean, every year that sickness returns, the same problem returns, and you are in a vicious cycle. Today, in the name of Jesus Christ of Nazareth, I command that stubborn sickness or situation to be terminated NOW! You are now freed in the name of Jesus. AMEN!

CHAPTER SEVEN

HE ORDERS MY STEPS IN THE PATHWAY

I n my book *After His Touch*, I detailed my experience when I survived the massacre that took the lives of scores of innocent men and women, especially men, young men in the Fasayeazu Zorzor Lofa. I would like to further detail my experience of how I made it to safety the day after surviving nearly being beheaded and gunshots.

I will share this portion describing how He orders my steps in the pathway. Of course, I am talking about my pathway to safety. It is a complete miracle that I sit here today. I miraculously survived that night after an attempt to behead me, shoot, and stab me several times. Through God's powerful intervention, I was left in an unfamiliar forest to die and disappear without a trace. I was in deep pain, bleeding from the deep wounds in my neck in pain and from my back, where I was stabbed multiple times. Of course, there was no way to sleep that night due to the horror I was going through. I wept and prayed all night, seemingly all alone, as there was no one in sight to aid me.

Meanwhile, after my prayer in the morning, the Lord said to me, "Go to Guinea; there you will find safety." There was no doubt I desperately needed safety, but my big question was: How do I get to safety as I had never been to Guinea, nor was I familiar with the road that led to Guinea from the forest? After pondering this for a while, the Lord said to me again, "Go!" And at that juncture, I obeyed and took the road. It was March 1993 in the hot sun and the scorching heat of the dry season of West Africa. I was bleeding profusely and in severe pain, but I mustered the courage to push to safety as God graced me to keep walking, irrespective of the circumstances that had the propensity to prevent me from going any further.

As tears from my eyes and blood from my body were dropping to the ground, I was engulfed with severe pain and in the middle of nowhere. But, even there and in that situation, the invisible right hand of God was holding my hand and leading me to safety. Scripture declares, "*For I am the Lord your God who takes hold of your right hand and says to you, Do not fear; I will help you.*" (Isaiah 41:13 NIV).

In this Scripture, God promises to hold your hands even in the worst of scenarios, regardless of what you are going through. If you believe, you will experience the power of his mighty right hand, as I experienced 31 years ago when I was swept into safety, irrespective of all the odds.

I remember walking all day from morning to approaching evening hours, and finally, my sight caught some people on their farm. When they saw me, I remember they were initially afraid to come around me as I was soaked with blood and tears. Eventually, when they realized I was alone and appeared without weapons, they knew I needed to be rescued. At that juncture, they immediately came to my rescue, and just so you know, I was on Guinean soil. Finally, I arrived at the place I considered my rescue country.

The Guineans were so nice to me that they brought me to their village. But one thing they could not do was to keep me without the knowledge of the Guinean army at the border, and that was because of my physical condition; I needed urgent medical attention. The fact that I had to be taken to the Guinean army opened another challenge that needed God's intervention.

CHAPTER EIGHT

WONDERS OF HIS FAVOR

"This is what the LORD says: the people who survive the sword will find favor in the wilderness; I will come to give rest to Israel."

JEREMIAH 31:2

This Bible verse speaks directly to the heart of my situation as I was going through a defining moment in my life. I had survived the sword and gunshots, but I landed in a foreign country, helpless and at the mercy of ruthless military men at the Guinean border who had a record of killing fleeing Liberian men and young men who were perceived to be fighters entering their country. At this critical juncture, I desperately needed the favor of God to survive, and He stepped in just when I needed it.

Jeremiah declares the Word of God that those who survive the sword will find favor in the wilderness or the desert, as indicated by other translations. Of course, I found myself in the desert place in a strange country with a language barrier and a hostile army with a history of executing those perceived rebels entering their country. Nevertheless, here I was with machete wounds all over my body, soaked in blood, but unable to communicate to the army how I got the wounds and how I ended up there.

In the end, the Lord granted me unusual favor as I found favor with one of the military guys called Commando, who was considered one of the most ruthless army personnel at that post. Instead of killing me, Commando took it upon himself to mobilize able men in the town to transport me to the nearby city for medical attention. They brought a hammock, laid me in it, and crossed a long stake through it, and I was transported in it from village to village. Typically, in remote towns and villages where there is no vehicle for modern transportation, the people will use the hammock to transport the sick to the hospital. Commando was so restless that night as he ran ahead to every approaching village to mobilize fresh strength to continue the journey at the pace he wanted.

At this point, I had stopped talking and eating I remembered bread was brought for me to eat, but I was unable to eat. It was the second night running without any medical assistance, but God was in charge as He kept me going on supernatural life support. It's astonishing how the Lord granted favor to me to a man who was feared but not surprised because Scripture also reveals that the heart of kings is the hand of God. *"The king's is in the hand of the Lord, as the rivers of water: He turneth it whithersoever He will."* (Proverbs 21:1 KJV)

Due to the uncommon favor of God, Commando and his

recruits had no rest until, at midnight, we arrived at the Koinyama hospital in Guinea. Meanwhile, because it was so late and hardly any doctors or nurses were on duty, I was laid on an iron bed without any mattress. And that was my situation until the day broke when the medical workers came to the clinic. However, by this time, my appointed guardian, Commando, and the men who brought me to the hospital had left for their villages, and I was left alone with no one to present my case that morning officially.

DIVINE ARRANGEMENT

We must understand that there are times when God divinely arranges circumstances for our good. He orders our steps and strategically sends and places people ahead of us for our good. In the case of Joseph's brothers, the future Israelis, God sent Joseph ahead of them, even though it was through peculiar and adverse circumstances. However, all was in the plan of God for Joseph to go ahead of them in that tragically sad and painful form. In God's divine plan and fashion, Joseph's suffering and trials aimed to position him in a place of power and authority at the right place and time. He was there to help his family when they desperately needed help.

He sent a man before them, even Joseph, who was sold for a servant: Whose feet they hurt with fetters: he was laid in iron: Until the time that his word came: the word of the LORD tried him. The king sent and loosed him; even the ruler of the people, and let him go free. He made him lord of his house, and ruler of all his substance.

PSALMS 105:17-21, KJV

As for me, after I was brought to the clinic on that fateful night by Commando and his men, it was so late at night that there was no paperwork done for my admission. I was laid on a bed without a mattress, save a cloth that was laid on it to cushion it somewhat for my wounds, before laying me on it. The next big challenge was that Commando left immediately after delivering me at the clinic, which meant I was on my own the following day as the health workers began to show up at work.

In the morning hours, there was the question of who brought me to the clinic, my identity, and other details, but there was no one to identify me. During that time, there were stories of wounded individuals who crossed over from Liberia to escape the war but who were perceived to be combatants. They were left to die because fighters or rebels weren't even allowed to cross the border.

Meanwhile, while this confusion about my identity was going on the third day after my great and miraculous escape, I was unable to say a word due to my injuries and the pain I was enduring; someone showed up. In the clinic that morning was a lady who had crossed over from Liberia with her daughter. I am told that she gave birth at the same clinic. The lady was a member of our church in Liberia. She decided to enter the room I was kept in to see the perceived combatant, who was not being attended to due to suspicion. Praise God! Because when she entered, she recognized me and told the medical people that I was not a combatant but a minister of the Gospel and that she was a part of our church in Liberia. That is when my condition changed, as they began to treat me with respect and attend to my medical needs. As the hours and day passed, a few more Liberian refugees arrived who knew me and corroborated the testimony of the first lady.

I am so grateful the Lord positioned this lady at the clinic that day for His glory, as I was hours away from giving up. But her testimony changed the narrative as I was giving medical treatment.

As I close this chapter, I am led to pray for the one reader right now:

Heavenly Father, I pray that whoever reads this book will experience divine arrangements as you did for me 31 years ago. I pray that You would send men and women ahead of them to be destiny helpers positioned in higher and lower places where they are needed to enhance their destinies, breakthroughs, and diverse miracles and testimonies. May they not meet evil men in times of need but generous men of goodwill who will do everything to help catapult them to their next levels, seasons, and chapters of life. In the mighty name of Jesus, I pray. Amen!

CHAPTER NINE

FAITH THAT MOVES YOUR MOUNTAINS

And Jesus said unto them, Because of your unbelief: for verily I say unto you, If ye have faith as a grain of mustard seed, ye shall say unto this mountain, Remove hence to yonder place; and it shall remove; and nothing shall be impossible unto you.

MATTHEW 17:20, KJV

As we begin to draw the curtain on these powerful and life-changing revelations and testimonies, I am inclined to talk to you about faith, which is the catalyst that powered the move of God in my life over the years. Scripture declares that without faith, it is impossible to please God.

In Matthew 17:20 Jesus describes faith as a seed. In fact, it's not just a seed but a mustard seed. It's interesting to note that the mustard seed is considered the smallest of all seeds! How then, can the smallest of all seeds, as described by Jesus, be so powerful to remove a mountain? There is a lesson for us to learn here, and we must understand it.

First, it is essential to acknowledge that your faith is your seed. Acknowledging this puts you in the position of a cognizant farmer who understands that a single seed in his or her hands, no matter its size, can produce a miraculously abundant harvest. I have seen people who fail to acknowledge their faith but rely on the faith of others to cause a harvest for them.

You must acknowledge that your faith will see you through that situation, no matter its size. The Bible teaches us that people perish because of the lack of knowledge. This is in no way teaching spiritual pride or arrogance. It is Biblical for us to have faith partners, prayer partners, whatever you term it, but your seed of faith is the catalyst to your breakthrough.

Jesus often told those he healed, "Your faith has made you whole." He didn't say my faith has made you whole, but "your" faith. It is clear here that, occasionally, the Master's faith played a critical role in those healings and miracles. However, the seed of faith is in your hands. Acknowledge, accept, believe, and put it into action. It's time you stop running after miracle workers and prophets, knowing that you have, in your hands, what it takes to get the miracle you are seeking.

31 years ago, at age 17, when rebels came to my village to massacre us, their arrival alone was a fearful event. But, to make matters worse, they called on everyone to come out of our houses; that if we didn't come out, we would be killed if they had to enter to retrieve us. People began to jump out of their houses immediately. I did not have a machete, an AK-47, or an RPG that rebels were carrying that night. But I had a weapon more powerful than they possessed. I had a seed of faith.

With my seed of faith, I overcame the fear that was released in the village that night, and I remained focused on not hurriedly coming out and being butchered mercilessly. With my seed of faith, I stood still and saw the power of God at work. With my seed of faith, after 31 years, I am here in the land of the living, imparting this faith and trust in God to my generation.

In the conclusion of the Gospel of Mark, which is considered the Gospel of action or the gospel of miracles, the Apostle Mark reminded us of Jesus' teaching saying:

> *And, these signs shall follow them that believe; In my name shall they cast out devils; they shall speak with new tongues; They shall take up serpents; and if they drink any deadly thing, it shall not hurt them; they shall lay hands on the sick, and they shall recover.*
>
> MARK 16:17-18, KJV

The lesson learned from this Scripture is that you will be followed by miracles or signs and wonders if you acknowledge the least of faith in your hands.

CAST YOUR SEED FAITH

It is one thing to acknowledge that your faith is a seed in your hands and yet another thing to put it to work: you must cast it into the soil for it to work for you. Unless your seed is released into the ground, it will never germinate, grow, and cause a miraculous harvest for you. In Matthew 17:20, Jesus says if you have faith as a grain of mustard seed, you will say to this mountain, move from here to there. Notice in this verse that Jesus first talks about having the seed, and then, he says you will say to this mountain, which speaks to the casting of the seed. It's not just that you have the seed faith, but you cast it by putting it to work. Once it is put to work, mountains will give way.

The Apostle James strongly emphasized casting the seed of faith when he said, "*Even so faith, if it hath not works, is dead, being alone.*" James 2:17. It is not enough for the farmer to have seeds in his storehouse and expect a harvest; he or she needs to step out into the fields, cultivate the land, cast the seed, and wait for the harvest. On the fateful night of the massacre, having faith alone wasn't enough for my survival. I had to put it to work by lying flat on my belly and saying, "I shall not die but live." I also said, "Yea, though I through the valley of the shadow of death, I will fear no evil." Finally, I got up and stepped out in faith in the presence of the bloodthirsty rebels and came out alive. Step out today in faith and put your faith to work.

CONCLUSION

As I conclude this testimonial book, it is my wish that many will be blessed from it in fulfillment of the Word of God that says, *"And they overcame him by the blood of the Lamb, and by the word of their testimony; and they loved not their lives unto the death."* (Revelation 12:11, KJV)

Section B of this verse says, *". . . and the word of their testimony . . ."* Pay attention to what God's word is saying here. We become victorious when we look back and acknowledge and appreciate the goodness of God in our lives and the lives of others in the past, believing that he can replicate or even do bigger things in our lives.

In the Old Testament, the word "testimony" derives from the Hebrew "'êdûth," which means "do it again." Therefore, testimonies reveal what we expect God to do again. If He did it yesterday, He can do it again. The sharing of testimonies encourages and profoundly imparts the faith of others, consequently releasing the power of God to do similar miracles or exploits.

As you have taken time to go through this book unraveling the profound imparts of God on my life and the lives of those mentioned in this book, you are at the tipping point of experiencing your miracle if only you believe. The power of testimonies is inarguable. You can disagree with me on many fronts, but you cannot disagree with what God has done in my life. It is a personal experience. The evidence of His miracles and exploits is visible and inarguable. The Hebrew writer puts it right when he says,

"*Jesus Christ, the same yesterday, today, and forever.*" Hebrews 13:8. If he did it yesterday, he can do bigger things today.

Let's conclude with this prayer.

Heavenly Father, we believe in your word, "Jesus Christ, the same yesterday, today, and forever." I pray that those reading this book encounter the exploits and wonders needed in their lives. May the life of the person reading this book never remain the same due to the faith released into their spirit through these astonishing testimonies that will bring down mountains, tear down walls, and open iron gates. I declare the healing of all manner of sicknesses and diseases that this reader is experiencing. Just as you have heard of the outstanding healing wonders contained in this book, so will be your portion in the mighty name of Jesus, as your testimonies shall be heard very soon. AMEN!

ABOUT THE BOOK

Wonders in the Pathway is a testimonial book that unravels God's inexplicable natural wonders and exploits. These testimonies range from biblical history to some astonishing miracles seen in God's natural creations, in Jesus's ministry, and in the personal life of his servant, Pastor David Saa Fatorma, Jr.

Pastor Saa Fatorma encountered Christ as a youth and witnessed the incredible move of the right hand of God in his personal life and ministry.

The book sheds light upon the power of testimonies, with the hope that the reader's faith will reach a tipping point that orchestrates their miracle. Testimonies are powerful tools for overcoming one's huddles. This book brings you true life experiences and personal encounters that have the propensity to change your life forever, just as the testimonies contained here have imparted and inspired so many lives over the years across the globe.

You will do yourself well by grabbing a copy and finding time to discover the breathtaking wonders of God found in this book. You can be assured that your life will never remain the same as you read. SHALOM!

ABOUT THE AUTHOR

Pastor David Saa Fatorma, Jr. is the General Overseer of the Light Streams Chapel Solution Outreach Ministries. He is married to Veronica, and they are blessed with five children. He has planted several churches across Liberia and provides leadership for few church networks in Liberia.

He is a media personality as he broadcasts the Word of God on radio stations across Liberia weekly. He also runs teaching programs on TV, the Notable Streams Hour, Sunday morning teachings, and Voice of the Church, which discusses socio-political, economic, religious, and trending national issues from an unbiased and biblical perspective. He holds a Master's degree in Theology. He is also an international conference speaker who has traveled to several countries worldwide, including the USA, the UK, Australia, and many African countries, preaching the Gospel of Jesus Christ.

Pastor David Fatorma is a survivor of a massacre that happened during the 15-year civil war in Liberia and has authored two books: *After His Touch* and his recent book, *A Prophetic Call for National Shifting*.

David Saa Fatorma, Jr., is a humanitarian and philanthropist who founded and leads the Leadership and Education for Africa Project (LEAP, www.leapsponsorship.com), with US and UK links. Most recently, the president of Liberia, His Excellency Joseph Nyuma Boakai Sr., picked Pastor David Saa Fatorma, Jr., as his successor as chairman of his foundation, the Joseph Nyuma Boakai Foundation, a nonpolitical, nongovernmental, and non-profit humanitarian organization.

9 798888 981634